T0130455

The Purple Watermelon

Stephanie L. Jensen

© 2010 Stephanie L. Jensen. All rights reserved.

No part of this book may be reproduced, stored in a retrieval system, or
transmitted by any means without the written permission of the author.

AuthorHouse™
1663 Liberty Drive
Bloomington, IN 47403
www.authorhouse.com
Phone: 833-262-8899

Because of the dynamic nature of the Internet, any web addresses or links contained in this book may have changed
since publication and may no longer be valid. The views expressed in this work are solely those of the author and do
not necessarily reflect the views of the publisher, and the publisher hereby disclaims any responsibility for them.

Any people depicted in stock imagery provided by Getty Images are models,
and such images are being used for illustrative purposes only.
Certain stock imagery © Getty Images.

This book is printed on acid-free paper.

ISBN: 978-1-4520-1417-3 (sc)

Library of Congress Control Number: 2010905367

Print information available on the last page.

Published by AuthorHouse 02/26/2022

authorHOUSE®

To Janessa, Ryker, Jaden, Bryken, MaKenna, Kelby and Briggs.
Thanks for bringing so much imagination into my life.
Love you, Stebbers.

To my wonderful friends, supportive Mother and Father,
the love of my life,
and to a little boy named Lakai and his mom.
May you always feel loved.
Summer

One spring morning Matt awoke to the sweet tunes of the birds singing outside his bedroom windows. He blinked his eyes once, only to feel his dog, Scott licking his ears as if he didn't need an alarm clock to wake him up to greet the day.

Matt got up from his warm bed, put on his favorite blue shirt and walked outside into the gentle cool air of the spring morning to help his father do chores before heading off to school.

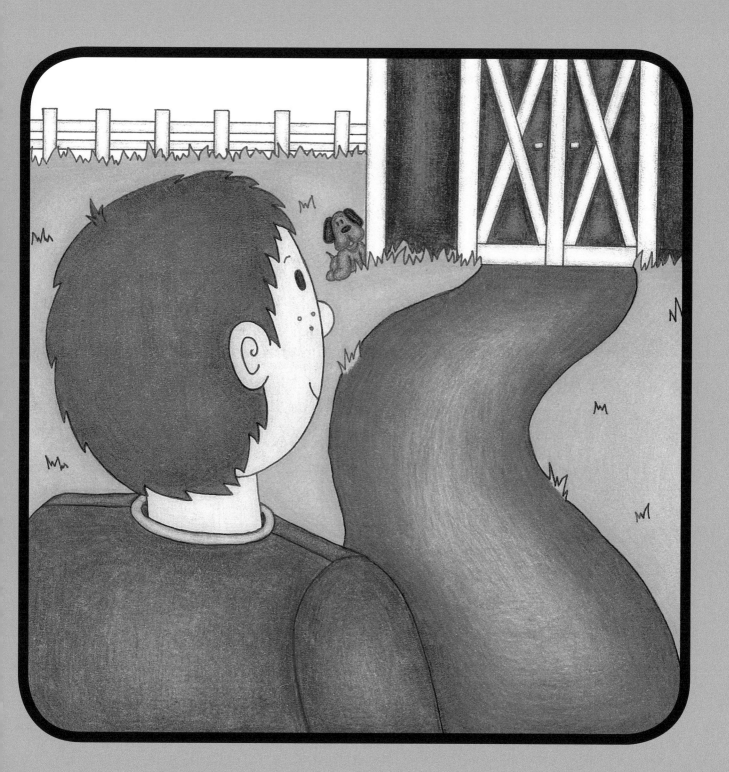

Matt loved scooping up the green hay into the pitchfork and challenging himself to see how far he could throw the hay into the fields for the horses to eat.

He loved chasing the chickens into the pens only to find a dozen eggs waiting to be gathered and brought into the house to use for scrambled eggs, yummy cakes and treats.

Matt and his sister Amy were the best of friends. Because Amy was a few years younger than Matt, she became his shadow when it came to helping on the farm and walking to and from school. Together they would discover crawly bugs, odd-shaped rocks and interesting things that they called treasures.

One afternoon Matt and Amy were walking home from school when Matt noticed something small and shiny mostly tucked under a bush.

"Hey Amy," said Matt, "Look under that bush. Can you see something shiny?" Amy blinked her eyes a couple of times until they focused in on the shining seeds hidden far under the bush.

"Matt," Amy replied, "Let's get a closer look to see what is making those seeds so shiny."

Amy took a hold of Matt's hand and together they walked with caution over to where the objects laid on the ground. When Matt and Amy came closer to the seeds, what they saw was unbelievable!

Matt said to Amy with excitement in is voice, "Look at the shiny seeds! Let's take some home and plant them to see what will grow."

Amy reached inside of her backpack and pulled out an old sack that was left over from school lunch. "Matt, help me put some seeds in this sack," Amy said while being very careful not to take all the seeds at once.

"We can take these seeds home and plant them in the ground to see what will grow," Amy said with excitement in her voice.

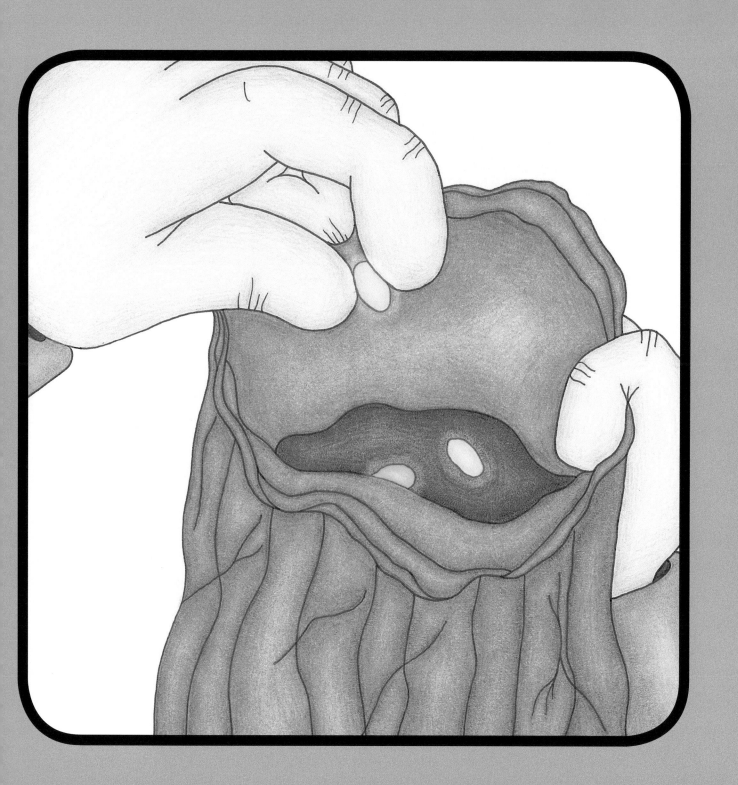

Matt's thoughts wandered off into the sky as he daydreamed about what the seeds could grow into. He noticed Amy was also staring off into space.

When they reached their farm, Matt said, "Amy you go and get a bucket of water and I'll get the shovel to dig a hole."

Matt and Amy met over near the old tire swing. "Amy, you hold the seeds while I dig the hole. Then when I tell you, place the seeds side by side in the hole." Amy did as she was instructed and then together the children covered up the seeds with the warm dirt and the cold water. Then they stood together watching and waiting for the seeds to grow.

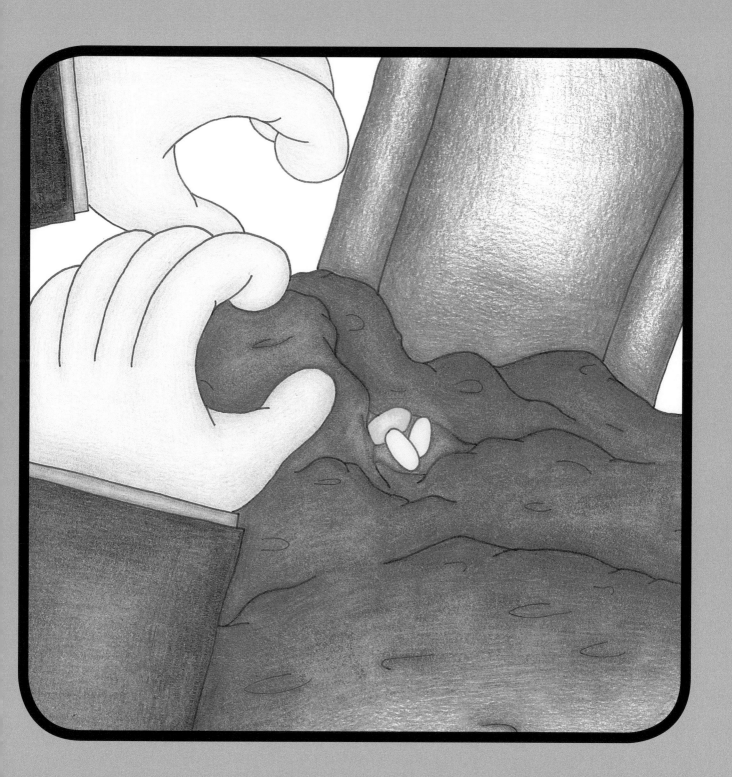

Spring ended and summer came in full blast with warm temperatures and humidity that required lots of cool air and icy drinks to endure the hot months ahead. Matt and Amy were closely tending their small garden that consisted of three odd looking seeds, growing from the ground.

One particularly hot summer day Matt said to Amy, "It's your turn to water the seeds, remember?!"

Amy looked up at Matt with her hands on her hips and said, "No, Matt, I watered them yesterday. It's your turn!" Matt got a frustrated look in his eyes and said, "Amy, it's not just my responsibility to always water the seeds. You have to take a turn also! Besides, you are the one that wanted to take the seeds home so it's not my job to water them!"

Days turned into weeks. Matt and Amy forgot all about watering the seeds.

One warm evening Matt and Amy were playing a game of basketball outside, trying to soak in as much of the summer as they could before school started again. Amy was dribbling the ball when Matt shouted to her in his big brother voice, "Pass the ball to me so I can make a shot." Amy passed the ball to Matt, but the ball went way over his head. He jumped high in the air to catch the ball.

The basketball tipped his fingers and went right into a dirt pile by the old tire swing. Matt ran over to where the ball had landed and then out of the corner of his eye he noticed a green vine growing out of the ground.

"Amy" Matt yelled, "Come quick!"

Both children stood side by side each other, their eyes big with surprise, as they admired the green plant that was growing from the spot where they had planted the seeds. They exclaimed in unison, "The magic seeds!"

"Let's give the plants some water and then leave them be," Matt said with authority in his voice.

The children were again caring for the plant together. They observed the plants every move as it changed daily from a small vine into something huge. One day Matt was outside tending to the magic vines when he noticed something strange and odd shaped growing from the vine.

"Amy, come and look at what is growing from the vines," Matt yelled to his younger sister, who was sitting on the porch petting Scott, the dog.

She ran over to where Matt was standing with a watering pail in hand.

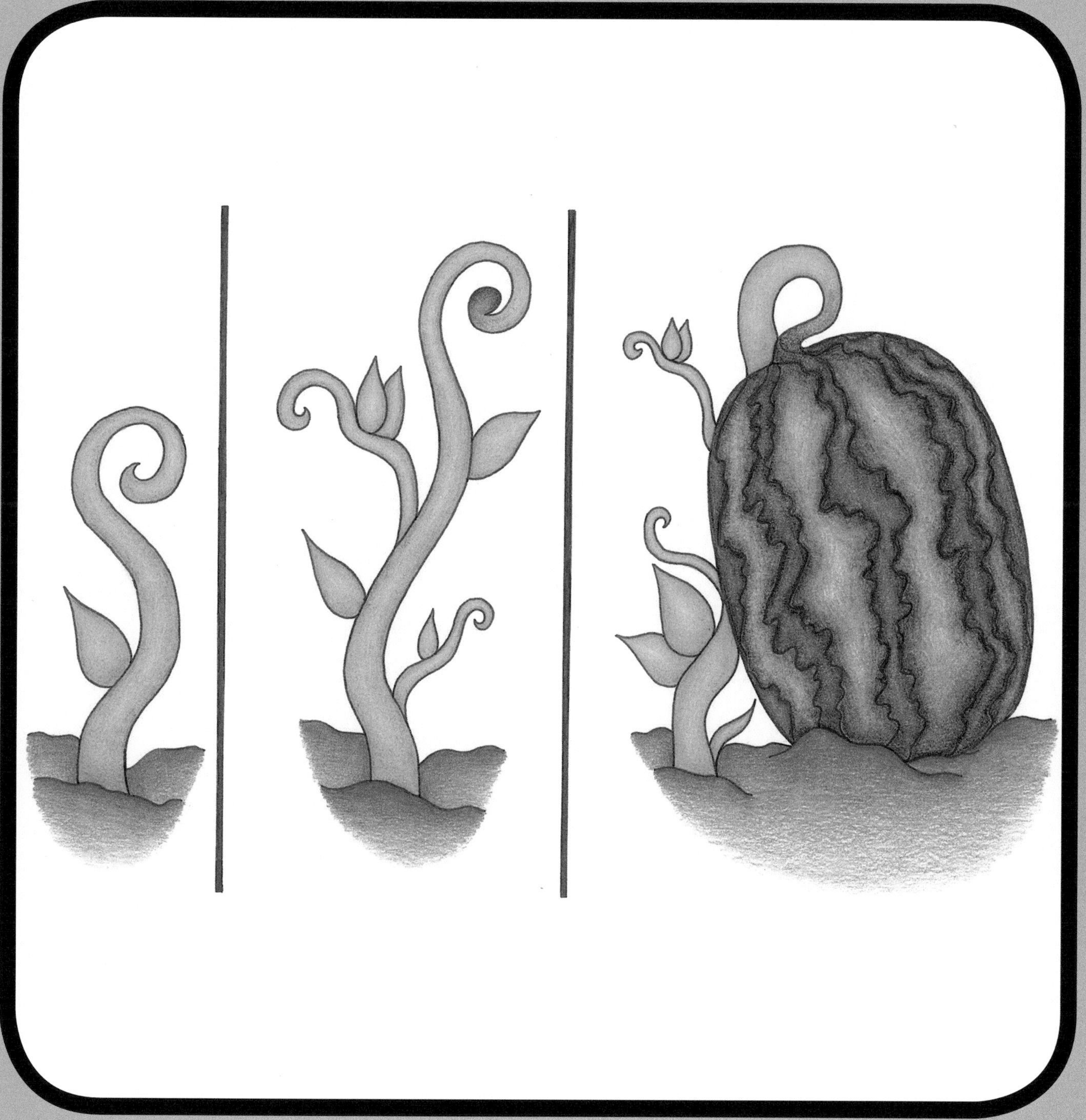

"Wow! Look at the purple odd shape balls growing from the vines. What are they?" Amy asked with curiosity in her voice. They marveled at the interesting color of the balls the seeds produced that were beginning to take the shape of a watermelon.

"Amy, this is not just an ordinary watermelon. This watermelon is purple!" Matt said with excitement in his voice. Amy's brown eyes became bigger as she looked up at Matt and said "What should we do, Matt?"

Matt scratched the side of his cheek as if that would make a thought appear and said,

"Let's pick one!"

Matt and Amy worked together to pick a purple watermelon from the vine. They pulled and tugged with all their might until finally the watermelon sprang from the vine, causing Matt and Amy to tumble backwards to the ground.

They took the watermelon into the house, wiped off the dirt to observe its bright purple color and then placed the watermelon on the kitchen counter.

Their four eyes were glued on the remarkable color and shape of the watermelon that they grew when Matt said with a trembling voice, "How about we cut it open to see what's inside and then we can each have a taste." Amy nodded in agreement as she carefully handed Matt the knife to cut into the watermelon.

He gently cut the bottom first and then worked his way up to the top of the watermelon, only to find that the knife wouldn't go any farther.

Matt asked Amy to help him break open the watermelon. Amy took hold of one side and Matt the other and together they ripped the two pieces apart to find purple ice cream packed firmly in the heart of the watermelon.

Matt looked at Amy with a surprised expression on his face as he said, "Amy, get us two spoons. Let's eat!"

As they sampled the purple ice cream they couldn't quite figure out what it tasted like, so they tasted the purple ice cream again and again until they decide it just tasted like purple ice cream packed in a watermelon.

What do you think the ice cream tastes like?

Printed in the United States
by Baker & Taylor Publisher Services